A Smooth Beginning:

20 Suggestions to Help Your Family Feel Settled in a New Country

Second Edition

by

Anne P. Copeland, PhD
The Interchange Institute

The
Interchange
Institute

The
Interchange
Institute

The Interchange Institute is a not-for-profit institution specializing in assisting families relocating globally. The Institute conducts research on the impact of intercultural transitions on individuals and families. From the results of this research, a variety of services are provided, including workshops and training, publications and products, and consulting services.

The Interchange Institute
617) 566-2227
www.interchangeinstitute.org

A Note of Introduction

Dear Reader,

So you are in the process of moving to a new country! Maybe you are planning to stay for only a few months, maybe for a very long time. In either case, the experience is sure to change your life in both expected and surprising ways. Living in a new culture always does.

During your first days in your new location, you will be making many decisions — some big (where to live), some small (where to shop). And so many things will be different — some obvious (language) and some small and subtle (how to cook on your new stove). It is easy to feel overwhelmed. Do not feel that you must make all important decisions in these first few weeks. Your most important job is to set up your home and family life in a way that is comfortable for all.

I have written this small booklet to help you during your first few weeks. It is about what you and (if you have one) your family can do to have a smooth beginning to your intercultural adventure. It is based on several assumptions, based on my own experience and on our Institute's research on families in intercultural transition:

- Moving to a new country almost always involves life-style changes that affect who does what in couples and families. If individuals can be flexible in taking on new roles (and giving up old ones), everyone benefits.

- People move to new countries for many reasons. Remember *your* reasons for the move (which may be different from your spouse's), and keep track of your progress in meeting your goals.

- Adjusting to life in a new country means finding a balance between new values and ideas, and values and ideas from your home country. Each family member will probably find a different balance between old and new — don't expect otherwise. The balance you choose may change over time. It will be helpful to your family if you talk together about your reactions to the new country and its culture as you encounter it.

So, here are 20 suggestions to help you and your family. You'll find some workbook activities in the sidebars on each page, to keep you focused on settling in quickly and smoothly.

Good luck and enjoy this wonderful opportunity.

Sincerely,

Anne P. Copeland, PhD

First Things First — Establish Your Routines

1. Eat and sleep well. Researchers have shown clearly that adults and children who go through more changes and stresses are more likely to get physically ill than people who do not. In the days surrounding your move, you will be very busy setting up your new home, and may not eat or sleep very well. Emotions will be very strong. Excitement, sadness, relief, happiness, confusion, and worry are all common. Every job will feel more difficult if you are tired. Try hard to stay healthy. You cannot be helpful to your family if you are sick.

2. Help your children eat and sleep well. Make your children's bed and meal times as similar to home as you possibly can. If you do, your children will feel more comfortable and, so, eat and sleep better. For example, keep the same bed time. Read books from home, or if you did not bring any, read new ones in your home language. Whatever you did at home to get a child ready for bed, do here now. For a while, your children may want bed time to be as it was when they were younger. They may want to sleep with a favorite toy, or to have you read aloud to them. Understand that this is a normal way for a child to learn to be comfortable.

In the same way, try to make meal times familiar to children. If you can, make the

Our Routines

I am healthiest when I sleep _____ hours per night.

I function best if I eat:

_____

_____

_____

_____

Before bed time, my children always:

_____

_____

_____

_____

My children's favorite foods are:

_____

_____

_____

_____

My children usually eat meals
at:_____
      (time)
with: _____
_____
    (people)

I get exercise by:

_____

_____

_____

_____

The Same and Different

Parts of our routine that we can keep the same as at home:

_____

_____

_____

_____

_____

_____

_____

_____

_____

Parts of daily living that will be very different:

_____

_____

_____

_____

_____

_____

_____

_____

same kind of foods as you had at home. Or if this is not possible, keep the process of meal times the same — eat at the same time of day, sit in the same arrangement around the table, give the children the same chores of setting the table or washing dishes, etc.

I understand that in many ways, your sleeping and eating arrangements will be different in your new home than they were at home. And after you have lived in your new home a while, your family's meals and sleeping patterns may change even more. But in the first weeks, if you can find even a few ways to make sleep and food feel familiar to your children, they will be more likely to feel comfortable, and to stay healthy.

3. Make your new residence a "home." Until your residence starts to feel like your home, you will feel unsettled. People differ in what makes them feel settled. Our research shows that those who unpack their boxes, set up their kitchen, meet at least one neighbor, and hang or display photos and art work quickly are the ones who feel most settled, happiest and most loyal to their employer. You may have different tasks that are important to you – setting up a computer, finding a sports facility, figuring out where to buy food your family likes. Whatever it is, do what you need to do, soon.

4. Prepare ahead for emergencies. You will feel calmer if you have a plan for emergencies. In the back of this booklet is a page for emergency telephone numbers. In an emergency, it is easy to forget your new address, or the words you will need to make emergency calls in the host language. Take a few minutes now with your telephone book and fill in the telephone numbers for your town, and translate the emergency phrases. Then tear the last page out of this booklet and tape it next to your telephone. Teach your children how to use the telephone if you think they are old enough.

In many countries, there is a short, easy-to-remember telephone number that you can call in any kind of emergency — medical, fire, or crime. For example, in the US, it is "911." Learn the number in your area, teach it to your children, and tape it next to all the telephones in your home. Use this number only in a serious emergency. This service will send police, an ambulance, and/or fire truck as needed, or give you other advice.

Next, find the address of the nearest hospital. Know how to get there, using your car, a taxi, or public transportation.

Check your home for safety, just as you would at home. Pay particular attention to the parts of your new home, furnishings, and toys that are new for you and your children (see Sidebar). For example, if you have a

Making Our New Home Safe

In our new home, we have:

❑ a kind of gas or electric heater and/or stove that we have never had before

❑ balconies

❑ windows that children can open

❑ hot water that is very hot

❑ busy streets nearby

❑ bodies of water nearby

❑ a kind of electricity that we have never had before

❑ kitchen storage that is low enough for young children to reach

❑ some other potentially risky feature:

_____

Staying Safe in Our Community

The telephone number of our nearest consulate or embassy is:

_____

Registering our current address with our embassy is:
❑ required
❑ suggested

We have been advised that we should use caution when moving around:

❑ our neighbor-hood
❑ our route to school
❑ our route to work
❑ public transportation
❑ other:

_____
_____
_____
_____

new kind of electric appliance or heater, be sure you understand how to make it work safely.

Have two different plans for getting out of your home in case of fire. If your children are old enough, discuss these plans with them. Choose a place to meet outside so no one will re-enter a home looking for someone who is already outside.

Keep a list of all family members' cell/mobile telephone numbers in your wallet and/or coded in your own mobile telephone. Depending on where you are living, you may want to choose one central person to call in case of political or natural emergency.

5. Stay safe in your new community. Talk about safety with someone who is very familiar with your neighborhood and community — where you live, where your children will go to school, where you will work, where you will shop, and the routes from one to another. Ask whether it is safe for you and your children to walk alone. Ask about the need to lock doors and windows. Ask about whether public transportation is safe at all times.

Especially if you are now living in a country where there is tension with your home nation, take steps to blend in to your new community. You may want to dress like locals and avoid displays on your house that signal your nationality (like flags or signs). If someone taunts you, ignore him/her and walk away quietly.

Register with the local embassy or consulate from your home country when you are settled. (Find the number in your telephone book or on line.) In case of political or natural emergencies, it may be important for them to know where all citizens of their country are living. Put this telephone number into your speed-dial list on your mobile telephone.

US citizens can call The Office of Overseas Citizens Services, 888-407-4747, during business hours or 202-647-5225 evenings, weekends and holidays.

In A Political or Natural Emergency

For help during an emergency, my government's contact information is:

Name of Agency:

_____

Telephone Number:

_____

Website for information:

_____

My country's closest embassy or consulate is at:

Address:

_____
_____
_____

Telephone:

_____

Website:

_____

Our Goals

What I hope to gain from living in this country:

1) _____
_____

2) _____
_____

3) _____
_____

What my spouse hopes to gain from living in this country:

1) _____
_____

2) _____
_____

3) _____
_____

What I hope my children will gain from living in this country:

1) _____
_____

2) _____
_____

3) _____
_____

Next Most Important — Stay Focused on Why You Are Here

6. Ask yourself if you are reaching your goals. Most people who move to a new country have some hopes about what their life there will be like. You may hope that your move will result in improved career possibilities. Or more time with your spouse and children. Or that you and your children will learn a new language. Or that you will all benefit from exposure to a new culture. You may hope to be free of pressures at home. Or you may be hoping to use the time to pursue an interest or skill. Families that keep these goals in sight often have an easier adjustment.

Write down the two or three most important goals you have for your move. Compare your list with that of your spouse and children. Once a month ask yourself if you have done something to help you meet each goal.

7. Find something about life in your new location that is fun for each family member — and do it. This is an especially good idea if there are members of your family who are not happy about moving. I do *not* mean that you should do special and exotic activities to make someone less unhappy. Instead, try to find a part of everyday life that will be better here than at home, and make sure it happens. Maybe your teenager can have more freedom here than at home. Maybe a neighbor has a child who can be a playmate for your pre-school child. Maybe one parent is home for children's bed time for the first time. Maybe one spouse has time to pursue a new hobby, avocation, or fitness goal. Maybe you can have a new level of involvement in your child's school. Be flexible — it may be that what is good is not familiar to you and it will take a while to discover it. If you can state aloud what these benefits are, it may help to keep them central.

8. Be proud of your ability to do new things. Write down all the things you did in the past week that you never did at home. Maybe you cooked a food you've never seen before. Or rode a new kind of transportation. Or went to a business party. Or earned money. Or worked but did not earn money. Maybe you prepared a school lunch for the first time. Or spent all day playing with your child. Perhaps you ordered your spouse's meal at a restaurant. Or your child ordered your meal for you.

Realize that every one of these accomplishments is impressive. When you try new activities, you are practicing "role flexibility" and this is extremely important for family adjustment. Be proud of how many new activities you have done — *even if they seem to be a setback to you.* Looking at your list of new activities will also help you understand why you feel stressed and tired.

My New Skills

10 things I have done here that I had never done before:

1) _____

_____

2) _____

_____

3) _____

_____

4) _____

_____

5) _____

_____

6) _____

_____

7) _____

_____

8) _____

_____

9) _____

_____

10) _____

_____

Steady as a Rock

Things that have not and will not change no matter where we live:

1) _____

_____

2) _____

_____

3) _____

_____

4) _____

_____

5) _____

_____

6) _____

_____

7) _____

_____

8) _____

_____

9) _____

_____

10) _____

_____

9. But let your children know that some things will remain the same. At the same time, try to give your children the sense that the most basic structure of their lives has *not* changed. Many family rules and values are the same. How family members speak to each other is the same. Family decision-making is the same. Your concern for them is the same, even if you are distracted by the move. These *may* change, of course, as your children get older and as you spend more time in a new culture — that is part of being a flexible family. But in the early weeks, it will be comforting to your children to feel that their family life is familiar.

Help Each Family Member Stay Connected to Your Home Culture

10. Stay in touch with home. Your friends and family will want to hear from you and hear about your new life. Technological advances make this easier every year.

If you choose to communicate in writing, at least sometimes, you will (a) have a record of your experience forever, for yourself, (b) get the benefit that comes from thoughtfully narrating your experience, and (c) be able to describe things once and share with your circle through technology. Remind your children that this is true for them, too. Write one long detailed letter/email, telling everything that has happened, how your family is adjusting, what you like and what you don't. Include [digital] photos as illustrations. Then either send your writing to everyone on your list, as is. Or go back and edit it for each person, adding or deleting particular details to suit their interests. Don't forget to send/keep a copy for yourself!

Writing could also include setting up a blog (a web log or on-line diary) where you write information about yourself and your experiences for people to read on the internet. Your blog can be open for anyone to read or just for people who request a password from you. Blogger.com and wordpress.com are two resources for information on setting up a blog.

My Circle

People I want to stay connected to:

1) _____
2) _____
3) _____
4) _____
5) _____
6) _____
7) _____
8) _____
9) _____
10) _____
11) _____
12) _____
13) _____
14) _____
15) _____
16) _____
17) _____
18) _____
19) _____
20) _____

My Plan

I will probably want to communicate with friends and family at home about:

❑ emergencies

❑ emotional support

❑ practical help

❑ sharing our experiences

❑ hearing about their lives

❑ my or their work

❑ child raising

❑ family members' health

❑ current political events

❑ the future

❑ our experience living in this country

❑ other:

_____

_____

_____

If you choose to communicate by telephone, be sure to investigate the growing number of options for making the calls inexpensively. For example:

• Ask if your telephone service offers an international calling plan; sometimes rates are especially low if you pick one country for most of your calls.

• Use a pre-paid telephone card.

• Use a mobile telephone service that allows international calls at affordable rates.

• From the US, use a 10-10 number which allows you to make international calls using your local telephone service. Compare options at 1010phonerates.com.

• Make free international calls using your computer, a headset, and free downloads (for example, www.skype.com). Some instant message systems now offer the option to have free "voice conversations," in some cases with live video using a web camera. Some options include Tango (tango.me) or Yahoo messenger (messenger.yahoo.com) or Google talk (google.com/talk)

If you are planning to make international telephone calls, think about how often and how long you will talk. Family members may have different ideas about what is most satisfying — some may find short but frequent calls the best; others may find those frustrating and prefer longer, less frequent ones.

If you find that you or your children spend a lot of time e-mailing or telephoning home, do not worry, at least for a few months. They/you are learning how important friends are and how to maintain friendships. Feeling good about social relations is an important part of making new friends. They/you will apply these lessons to making new friends in your new location. (However, please read Tip #13, too.)

11. Help every family member see some positive aspects to both the host and home cultures. Each member of your family will have different reactions to the host country. It is common for members of one family to like and dislike different things about living in the new culture. Sometimes, however, one spouse prefers everything about the home culture and the other spouse prefers everything about the host culture. Research on immigrant families has shown that this pattern is very hard on adults and children. Families in which all members value some aspects of both the home and host culture have an easier time adjusting.

So, talk often with your family about what you each like and do not like about living in your new location, compared with home. Do not try to convince family members that their negative perceptions are "wrong," but do try to help everyone see some positive aspects.

The Upside

Things that are better here for me:

_____

_____

_____

Things that are better here for my spouse:

_____

_____

_____

Things that are better here for my older/oldest child:

_____

_____

_____

Things that are better here for my middle child:

_____

_____

_____

Things that are better here for my younger/youngest child:

_____

_____

_____

Home Away from Home

Places we can speak our home language:

_____

_____

_____

Places we can find food from home:

_____

_____

_____

Places we can get news about our home country:

_____

_____

_____

Places we can hear familiar music:

_____

_____

_____

Places we can meet people of our religion:

_____

_____

_____

12. Find an activity for each family member that makes a connection to home. Adults and children will enoy the sense of familiarity and comfort that comes from being with others from the same culture. As your children spend more and more time away from your home, it will also be important for them to stay in touch with the language and values from home.

Start looking now for a home-culture activity that each family member will enjoy. Here is a brief list of ideas:

For children:

• attend after-school or weekend classes that teach your native language

• attend cultural heritage classes or clubs that teach about your home country's culture and history

For adults and children:

• subscribe to a newspaper or magazine from home, or reach news from home on the internet:

• play a sport that is common at home, even if you did not play it often when you lived there:

• attend a religious or cultural organization that is in your native language, and/or that includes many people from your country;

- learn to do traditional arts (music, dance, arts, crafts) from your home country;

- cook food from home;

- find at least one other friend from your country.

You may not be able to find a place to do your favorite activities (for example, play ice hockey in Egypt or grown tropical flowers in New York City). Think about the essence of what you love about the activities — perhaps that may be possible in your new location, for example, a different sport that provides great exercise and team spirit, or a different plant to grow in an urban garden.

Adapting My Goals

One thing I love to do at home is:

_____

_____

_____

I can't do this here, but I will look for an activity that also lets me:

_____

_____

_____

Making Friends

Understanding how you are accustomed to making friends can help you understand the process of making friends in your new country.

Think about a friend you made at home within the last 5-8 years.

Where and how did you meet?

_____

_____

_____

_____

Did the early days of your friendship involve more talking or more doing shared activities?
❑ talking
❑ doing

How long did it take before you felt like "friends?"

_____

(continued on next page)

Build Connections in Your Host Community

13. Find a local network of friends and acquaintances. Our research has shown clearly that people who have friends and acquaintances in their new host communities have better adjustment than those who rely exclusively on friends and family via email or international telephone calls.

Look for ways to make new friends. This can be frustrating if everyone you meet appears to be too busy with their existing friends to welcome you into their circle. Remember, too, that cultural values and habits influence how friendships develop. The pace of getting to know each other, how much self-disclosure is common, how much you rely on friends for help — these are all very different in different countries. You may be surprised (and hurt) by the reaction you get from host nationals you try to befriend. Before you take their reactions personally, consider that you are probably encountering a deep cultural difference that neither of you is aware of. Some ideas:

♦ make friends with people from your home country or some third country; while your intercultural experience will be richer if you eventually make host culture friends, you get very real empathy and support from people who are going through the same losses and surprises as you

- join a sports or fitness club that has group activities and a place to socialize as well as work out

- offer to help host nationals learn your native language by having conversation hours with them

- look for people in your host culture who are also looking for new friends, for example, because they just moved there (try a newcomers' club) or who share a life stage with you (for example, who have a new baby or recently launched adult children)

- look for organizations focused on your home culture; host nationals who are members may be especially interested in being friends with you

- volunteer your time at a school, cultural organization, service agency, historical site, or arts center; in the US, see **www.volunteermatch.org** or **www.servenet.org** for organizations looking for help

- invite your children's friends' families to your home or to share an outing with you

- take a class at a university or adult education center

14. Meet your neighbors. Even if they are not people who are likely to be close friends with you, you will feel more settled if you know the people living near you. They will also be a valuable resource to you if you

(continued from previous page)

How important were these in the development of that friendship:

❑ shared past experiences
❑ shared current experience
❑ shared language
❑ humor
❑ shared cultural history
❑ practical assistance for each other
❑ shared leisure activities
❑ our spouses or children were also friends
❑ shared world view
❑ other:

_____

_____

_____

_____

_____

My Children's Friends

Child 1 (____)
- ❑ tends to make friends easily
- ❑ tends to have one or two close friends rather than a group of friends
- ❑ is happy playing alone a lot of the time
- ❑ needs shared language to have fun with another child

Child 2 (____)
- ❑ tends to make friends easily
- ❑ tends to have one or two close friends rather than a group of friends
- ❑ is happy playing alone a lot of the time
- ❑ needs shared language to have fun with another child

need information about local safety, health, shopping, education, or entertainment issues.

Maybe your neighbors will come over to your home on the day you move in, carrying a small gift of food, ready to welcome you to the neighborhood. Sometimes this happens, but often it does not. You may live in a neighborhood where people are simply very busy and preoccupied with their lives, families, and old friends. Or, you may live in a very mobile community, where people move a lot. (In the US, 12-20% people have changed homes in the last year. Only 41% currently live in the same state as where they were born.) In this case, your neighbors probably do not expect you (or themselves) to become a permanent member of that community. And of course, in your case, it may be very true and clear that you are, in fact, only here for a short while.

Finally, your neighbors may be unsure about how to welcome you — They may be wondering, "Do they speak my language? And if not, how can I talk to them?" Or "What kind of food or gift would be appropriate to bring them — what if I bring the 'wrong' thing and insult them?"

Here are some suggestions for meeting neighbors:

• Look around to find out what the current

issues are in your community. When you meet people in a park, playground, or waiting room, ask them what they think. ("Why is the story about that politician so important?" Or "Could you please explain to me why everyone is so upset that the school fired the football coach?") People will be pleased that you care about your shared community.

• If you cook some food from your country, take a small plate of it to a neighbor you would like to know. Almost everyone likes to eat.

• Invite neighbors to your house, perhaps at a time of traditional celebration in your (or the local) country. I know one Swiss family living in the US who hosted the neighborhood Easter brunch every year; it was the first time some of them had met (!) and they all loved it.

15. Help your children make new friends too. If your children are pre-school age or if you have moved to your new location when school is not in session, you will have to look for children in your community.

Spend time where children play — playgrounds, pools, parks. These are places where new children might easily join in others' play, even if their host language is not so good.

Look for stores, libraries, or community cen-

(continued from previous page)

Child 3 (_____)
❑ tends to make friends easily
❑ tends to have one or two close friends rather than a group of friends
❑ is happy playing alone a lot of the time
❑ needs shared language to have fun with another child

Use this understanding of your children's friend-making style to help you know what kind of assistance they will need.

Finding New Friends

In the past, I have found people I enjoyed being with:

❑ by being introduced to them by a mutual friend

❑ at my job

❑ at a place of worship

❑ at a club where I was a member

❑ while doing volunteer work

❑ while doing a sport

❑ while involved in an arts activity

❑ at a meeting or concert

❑ in my neighborhood

❑ other:

_____

_____

ters with child-friendly play spaces. Start conversations with other parents by asking for information ("I just moved here. Can you tell me where the closest ice rink is?" "Is it safe for my 12-year-old to walk around alone here?")

If your children will be going to school, find out how common it is for there to be "new kids" at the school, especially those from other countries. Schools with lots of international families may have programs to introduce children to others, and will welcome input from different cultures into the school community easily.

On the other hand, if new kids from other countries are rare, they will have the benefit of being "special." Some children enjoy this status more than others. Talk with your children's teachers about how best to introduce them to the class in a way that makes them feel both noticed and included.

In the early days of your life in your new location, it may be more important for your children to feel comfortable with other children than to be learning academic material in school. Once they feel comfortable, they will be able to learn better. Try this:

• For younger children, spend time at the school after hours, in the playground. Informal play time, and simply being seen and becoming familiar, will help.

- Enroll your children in some after-school activities, like sports teams, chess teams, Scouts, or art clubs. Unlike school, in these settings, children are able to talk casually with each other, and friendships may grow more easily than at school.

- Invite other children to your house after school, or to go to a museum or other special place. Think about whether your child will do better in a larger group or with just one other child. Groups of three are hard for some children, as one child can be left out.

- Invite a whole family (including children who might be friends for your children) to your house, or to do an activity together. Sometimes children are more comfortable playing with new children if their families are there.

- Try to find ways to do your children's favorite activities. Adolescents, especially, miss being in situations where they excel. If you cannot find an exact activity match, look for one that shares some similarities. For example, find one that requires team cooperation (even if the sport is different) or artistic ability (even if the art or craft is different).

- If your child agrees, discuss social concerns with your child's teacher or the school guidance counselor. She/he may be able to give some advice or reassurance, suggest which children may be good friends

---

Where to Make Friends

Besides at school, my children may meet other children at the following places:

outdoor parks
_____
_____

after-school activities
_____
_____

sports facilities
_____
_____

family friends or neighbors
_____
_____

language school
_____
_____

other:
_____
_____

Hearing, Reading, Writing and Speaking

Every day I can hear my host language in the following places:

_____

_____

_____

Every day I can read my host language in the following places:

_____

_____

_____

Every day I can write in my host language in the following ways:

_____

_____

_____

Every day I can speak my host language in the following places:

_____

_____

_____

for your child, or tell you ways that your school can support friendships.

16. Learn the host language. The more comfortable you are in speaking the host language, the more authentic interactions with your host culture you will have. Adults with jobs outside their homes will surely practice their host language. And children in school will too. But it is often difficult for an adult without a job (especially one who has friends from the home country nearby) to find ways to practice the language. If you feel unsure of your abilities, you will naturally find it hard to talk with host nationals. This can make you feel lonely and, with time, isolated from the rest of your family.

So, if possible, join an adult-education class to practice your language. Hire a private tutor. Or, find out if your community has volunteer tutors who will help you for free. Read a local newspaper or parents' newsletter to practice local usage. Watch children's television, where the language level is usually easier. If available, set your television to display closed-caption text to accompany the audio broadcast. Try to find a way to speak and listen to the host language every day.

Here is some advice to help you help your child learn the host language:

• Continue to speak your native language at home, at least part of the time, even if learning the host language is very important to you. Children will learn a second language more easily if they are strong in a first. You need to ensure that they continue their language development in your native tongue.

• At the same time, be a role model for learning the host language for your children. Show them that you think learning the language is a good thing to do, and that you are willing to make mistakes in the process of learning.

• Look for ways your child can practice the language in private. It feels less risky to speak in small groups or to one other person.

• Don't be surprised if your children start to correct your language! They may learn it more quickly than you and will be proud of what they have learned.

• Understand that children often have a "silent period" when they first learn a new language — a time when they will not speak the language. This may last as long as six months, although it usually does not. Be patient. Your child is certainly learning to *understand* during this period, even if he/she is not speaking it. Some children wait until they can speak in complete, perfect sentences before they start to talk aloud.

• Remember that children who are learning

Places I Can Practice the Host Language

❑ with a friend or neighbor

❑ at my work

❑ while shopping

❑ while pursuing a hobby or sport

❑ by reading a local newspaper

❑ by watching local TV

❑ at a language class or with a tutor

❑ by watching local films

❑ at my children's school

❑ at a place of worship

❑ other:

_____

_____

_____

_____

_____

Good Reasons

Here are 10 things
I could do if I could
speak the host
language pretty well:

1) _____

2) _____

3) _____

4) _____

5) _____

6) _____

7) _____

8) _____

9) _____

10) _____

two languages at once are processing both languages, and may appear to be slower at speaking and reading than their friends. Do not panic. They are doing something more difficult. The reward will be knowing two languages and having a deep understanding of the function of language.

• Realize that it takes three to seven years to learn a language well. Your child may be speaking competently within six months or a year, but to function fully in school (or for you, in your adult life), it takes much longer.

• Older children may take longer than younger children to learn a new language. They are learning more complex language forms and more complex school material (math, science, history) at the same time as the new language. And, they may be more shy about speaking a second language in front of other people.

• There is an emotional aspect to learning a second language. If learning this new language has a positive tone to it — your child wants to learn, and you want him/her to learn it too — learning will be faster. Do not pressure your child or be critical of how quickly he/she is learning the language.

17. Explore your community's resources.
Unless you make a direct effort, it could take years to learn about all the resources in your new community. Knowing about these

resources, on the other hand, can lead you to language classes, places to meet new people, sports and arts facilities, health clinics, cultural events, and more. Try these:

• Go to your community's public library and ask if there are materials in your home language, or lists of classes and activities that interest you. Look on the walls for posters announcing events that interest you.

• Look in a telephone book or on the Internet for organizations that appeal to you. Search on-line using the name of your new community, the name of your home country, and your need ("Brookline, MA Japan children's activities").

Key Words

Keywords I will use in an Internet search for resources in my local community:

_____

_____

_____

_____

_____

_____

_____

_____

_____

_____

_____

Signs of Stress

Here is what we do or feel when stressed:

I:
- ❑ eat or drink more or less
- ❑ get sad
- ❑ get angry
- ❑ get critical
- ❑ get sick
- ❑ feel very tired
- ❑ other:

My spouse:
- ❑ eats or drinks more or less
- ❑ gets sad
- ❑ gets angry
- ❑ gets critical
- ❑ gets sick
- ❑ feels very tired
- ❑ other:

My children:
- ❑ act younger
- ❑ act up
- ❑ have school problems
- ❑ get sad
- ❑ get angry
- ❑ get sick
- ❑ other:

Prepare for Some Hard Times

18. Expect ambivalence. Feeling two opposite things at once is common in the first weeks and months in a new country (or longer!). There seem to be good parts to living in the new country (for example, it is exciting, or the weather is good, or the job pays well, or you have more time with your children). But there are bad parts too (for example, maybe one family member is very unhappy, or you are far away from a sick family member, or you haven't made friends, or you miss your job). Do not ask yourself — or your spouse or children — to feel completely positive all the time. Pressure to do so is likely to have the reverse effect.

19. Learn what "culture shock" is. Culture shock is a phrase that describes what people feel when they move to a new country (or culture). Culture shock takes many different forms. Some people feel very sad. Others feel angry. Some feel physically sick and blame the sickness on the new culture's water or food. Some children start to act like younger children (wetting their bed, or having nightmares). Some have behavior problems. Some stop doing well in school. Some people become very critical of their new culture and the citizens of that culture. Of course there may be other reasons for these changes. But do not underestimate the power of moving to a new culture.

Consider why moving to a new culture can be so difficult:

* If the host language is new for you, you will be spending your day trying to communicate your complex and interesting ideas through a language that is new and uncomfortable.

* Or, if you are fluent or a native speaker of the host language, when you speak you will assume that your listeners will interpret what you say in the way you meant. Remember that a common language often camouflages huge cultural gaps.

* Your day will be one ambiguous situation after another. In some cases, you will know that you do not understand what is happening. In others, you will think you understand what is going on and you will be wrong. Living with constant ambiguity is very tiring.

* It is also exhausting to live with so many new sensations — new tastes, sounds, sights, temperatures, sense of space, pace of life. Add to that all the new people you meet in a day and new kinds of decisions you have to make, and you will understand why you may feel tired.

* You may find that local stereotypes about your country are wrong. They may make you very angry and hurt.

* You will be in a minority in some ways — by

What's Hardest?

Put the numbers 1 through 5 next to the five things below that you find most challenging while living in your new location (1=the very most challenging):

___ communicating with others

___ not understanding the local systems

___ food

___ climate

___ our living conditions

___ locals' lack of understanding about me and my country

___ being an outsider

___ making friends

___ missing home

___ _____

___ _____

___ _____

___ _____

Understanding Why

I am confused or irritated when host nationals do this:

_____

_____

_____

but I understand they do it because:

_____

_____

_____

I am confused or irritated when host nationals do this:

_____

_____

_____

but I understand they do it because:

_____

_____

_____

your race, or language, or culture. It is common for people in minority positions to feel excluded, disempowered, ignored, and misunderstood.

• You are far away from the people who know and love you, and making new friends in a new culture, in a new language, takes time.

• Culture shock is usually not a sudden reaction to some dramatic event. Instead, it gradually becomes a problem, as a result of many smaller experiences. This means that you may be confused about why you feel upset — no one terrible thing has happened.

So do not be surprised if, after a few weeks or months of finding your new location a fun and exciting place to be, you wake up (or your child does) and want to go home. This is the common course of culture shock. First there is a period when living in a new country seems wonderful. Then culture shock hits. When this happens, it means you are really beginning to be involved in the local culture. You are no longer a tourist. After a time, adjustment improves, but there will still be cycles of feeling good and bad. Often, for those who return to their home country, there is a repeated phase of culture shock before they leave. And an even more surprising repeated phase when they get home.

20. Learn how to manage culture shock.

Culture shock takes many forms. You will not necessarily feel that your unhappiness or your child's problems are due to being in a new country. Consider that perhaps they are. Here are some actions you can take:

• It is better to acknowledge that some family member is having culture shock than it is to pretend that "everyone is fine." Children, especially, need to know that it is understandable and acceptable to feel some strain. If they know that their feelings are not too frightening for their parents, they will pass this phase more quickly. If you pretend that "everyone is fine," they may feel that their emotions are too frightening for you.

• Talk with your family and, if possible, a host national about your observations about what is the same and what is different in your new location. Practice stating your observations in a balanced, neutral way. Some locals will be better at talking about this than others. If your friend gets defensive (hurt or angry) at what you say, apologize and try re-wording your views. Or look for someone else.

• One of the best ways to live through culture shock is to "narrate" your experience as if you were a storyteller. Stand back and watch yourself. Many people do this in writing, in a journal or letter. Be as descriptive as possible. Do not assume that you know the motivation and inten-

How I Will Manage Culture Shock

I have done the following things to help me manage culture shock:

❑ read and completed side bar activities in this book

❑ noted the signs of culture shock for adults and children

❑ talked to family members about living in new country

❑ talked to a local about cultural differences

❑ learned about cultural values in new country

❑ wrote emails, letters, journal entries or a blog about living here

❑ did stress-reducing exercise

Celebrate

The things I am
proudest of about my
family's transition
are:

_____

_____

_____

_____

_____

_____

_____

_____

_____

_____

_____

_____

tion of the people you meet. Instead, describe what they do in specific terms. Then try to understand what has happened, based on your knowledge of the host culture. Most cultural behavior is rooted in some value. Often you will understand the abstract value, even if the behavior is irritating to you. This may help you understand people's behavior. For example, some people from other countries find Americans' informality to be disrespectful and intrusive. If you understand this informality as part of Americans' belief in equal opportunity, it may make it easier to hear.

Other Suggestions I Would Offer to Others

_____

_____

_____

_____

_____

_____

_____

About the Author

Dr. Anne Copeland is the founder and Executive Director of The Interchange Institute. She is a clinical psychologist with expertise in the issues families and individuals face when moving to new countries. From 1979-97 she was a faculty member in the Psychology Department at Boston University. She conducts research on individuals and families who relocate to new countries, and writes and speaks frequently about these issues. She has moved abroad and home again, with her husband and two daughters.

Additional Resources for International Newcomers

Please visit **www.interchangeinstitute.org** to order additional copies of this book and other useful materials, or to learn about our training and consulting activities.

Newcomer's Almanac and *English Practice Worksheet*
  A unique collection of information, advice, and cultural interpretation for international newcomers to the United States in a 12-page monthly newsletter. Targeted to meet the needs of individuals and families on temporary assignment or who have recently immigrated, *Newcomer's Almanac* is a transitional lifeline of practical tips and thoughtful analysis of American culture.

Hello! USA
  Practical information about American life and culture for international individuals and families traveling or moving to the U.S.

In Their Own Voice
  A collection of stories written by people who have moved to the United States from another country and culture. The writers describe the universal experience of those who find themselves in a new country, and reveal the intricacies and challenges of living and working across cultures.

Global Baby: Tips to Keep You and Your Infant Smiling Before, During, and After Your International Move (by Anne P. Copeland, Ph.D.)
  A short, practical guide to help you make an international move with an infant.

Research Reports
  Research on the process of moving to and living in a new culture is one of the central activities of The Interchange Institute. Download reports for free at www.interchangeinstitute.org

The Interchange Institute
www.interchangeinstitute.org
(617) 566 2227
orders@interchangeinstitute.org

Emergencies

Translate each of these Emergency Services now, so you do not have to do so in the middle of a crisis. Cut this page out of the booklet and keep it near your telephone.

	Translation	**Telephone**
Fire	_____	_____
Police	_____	_____
Ambulance	_____	_____
Poison Center	_____	_____

Nearest Hospital: _____

Be prepared to tell your address and telephone number. These may be hard to remember in the local language in an emergency, so translate them now and write them (in words, not numerals — "five five six two" not "5562") now.

My address is _____.
translation: _____.

My telephone number is _____.
translation: _____.

Here are some words you might need in an emergency. Translate them now, in a calm moment:

Please help me.   _____
Fire!   _____
Please send an ambulance. _____
My [husband] is very sick. _____
    ...wife...   _____
    ...baby...   _____
    ...mother...   _____
    ...father...   _____
    ...child...   _____
[name of any diseases or
conditions you have that
may require emergency care] _____

www.ingramcontent.com/pod-product-compliance
Lightning Source LLC
Chambersburg PA
CBHW060342290526
45793CB00003B/697